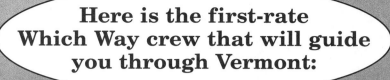
**Here is the first-rate Which Way crew that will guide you through Vermont:**

# Table of Contents

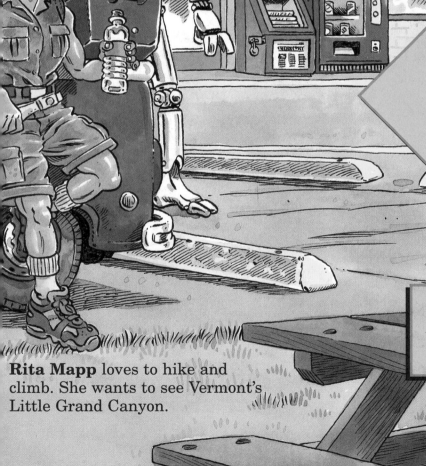

**CHIP**, the Which Way android, has his heart set on using his computer brain to inspect the fascinating patterns on some beautiful handmade quilts.

**Rita Mapp** loves to hike and climb. She wants to see Vermont's Little Grand Canyon.

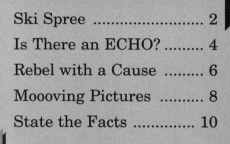

## WHO is heading for the WHICH WAY HALL OF FAME?

## WHAT will be in the WHICH WAY MUSEUM?

## WHERE will the WHICH WAY SUPERMAX MOVIE be filmed?

# SKI SPREE

You begin your adventure in the tiny town of Stowe. Mount Mansfield, Vermont's peak peak, is among the nearby mountains that make this one of the state's most famous ski resorts. The crew can't wait to hit the slopes. After grabbing their skis and snowboards, they ride the gondola to the ski trails.

By the end of the day, everyone has returned to the lodge except Hugh Tern. The Which Way driver is lost as usual. Help Hugh find the trail that leads to the ski lodge. Then schuss over to the bottom of page 3.

FINISH

Did you figure out which trail leads to the lodge?

**If it's trail 1,** cross off the SKIER.

**If it's trail 2,** cross off the WRITER.

**If it's trail 3,** cross off the PRESIDENT.

**If it's trail 4,** cross off the ACTIVIST.

Now go to page 28 and cross one person off your list.

# Is There an ECHO?

Hugh tosses his snowboard into the back of the Which Way van and gets into the driver's seat. He turns the van toward Burlington. Vermont's largest city is located on the shores of Lake Champlain. The crew heads straight to ECHO at the Leahy Center for Lake Champlain, the city's vibrant aquarium. ECHO stands for Ecology, Culture, History, and Opportunity. The aquarium is a great place to learn about preserving Lake Champlain and to see native wildlife and plants.

The aquarium is swimming with students from all over the state. Each student's sweat shirt tells the name of his or her hometown. Find the five kids with green shirts, then locate each town on your map. Write them, in order from north to south, on the list. After you do, head to the bottom of page 5.

**Don't Forget Your Map!**
All the towns can be found on your map of Vermont. You will find them near Interstate 91, which runs north and south through the state.

4

## LIST

**North**

Town #1 _____

Town #2 _____

Town #3 _____

Town #4 _____

Town #5 _____

**South**

Did you put all the towns in order from north to south? Each kid's shirt has a two-letter clue on it. Write these letters, in order, in the spaces below.

___ ___ ___ ___ ___   ___ ___ ___

Turn to page 28 and cross this famous Vermonter off your list.

5

# Rebel with a Cause

The Which Way crew waves good-bye to Lake Champlain and travels a short distance from downtown Burlington. Professor Pfeffer wants to visit the homestead of Ethan Allen, the leader of the Green Mountain Boys and a hero at the battle of Fort Ticonderoga during the American Revolution.

When the crew arrives at the Ethan Allen Homestead, they find a group of Vermonters dressed as Revolutionary War soldiers. They are acting out parts of a battle between the colonial and British armies.

A flyer describes what the costumed actors are doing. But some of the words are in code! To read it, replace each letter with the letter in the alphabet that comes two before it. (For example, a *C* would be replaced by an *A*.) When you finish, march to the bottom of page 7.

Soldiers had many chores between battles during time of war.

_ _ _ _ _ _ _ .
1

Some cleaned their OWUMGVU _ _ _ _ _ _ _ .
2

Others worked on their OCTEJKPI _ _ _ _ _ _ _ _ their horses.

The cavalry practiced TKFKPI _ _ _ _ _ _ .
3

Soldiers cleaned the heavy ECPPQPU _ _ _ _ _ _ _ before a battle.
4

Some soldiers filled canteens with YCVGT _ _ _ _ _ .
5

In their free time, soldiers sat near their VGPVU _ _ _ _ _ .
6

and wrote NGVVGTU _ _ _ _ _ _ _ home to their family and friend
7

Some soldiers liked to play ECTF _ _ _ _ games to pass the time.
8

6

Did you crack the code? Some of the letters have numbers underneath them. Write the letters in the correct spaces below.

___ ___ ___ ___ ___ ___   ___ ___ ___ ___ ___ ___ ___ ___
4   6   8   3   1   4     7   4   5   3   1   6   2   1

Cross this person off the list on page 28.

# Moooving Pictures

As the van heads southeast on Interstate 89, you pass field after field full of black-and-white cows. CHIP tells you that Vermont is known for its dairy farms. In fact, more than 40 percent of all the dairy products in New England come from the milk of these hard-working cows. Much of it is used to make butter, ice cream, and cheese.

The crew stops for a close look at the farm. While Rita and the Professor stretch, CHIP scans the pasture. The Which Way android has detected butter, ice cream, milk, and cheese in the scene. Can you spot them? Each item is hidden at least two times. Find them all, then check the clue on the bottom of page 9.

**Take away the activist.**

**Remove the writer.**

**Scoop out the two friends.**

**Rule out the politician.**

Have you found all of the hidden items?
One object is hidden *three* times. When
you find that object, look at the
instructions underneath it.
Turn to page 28 and put that
information to use.

# State the Facts

The crew rolls into Montpelier, Vermont's state capital. Professor Pfeffer mentions that Montpelier is the smallest capital city in the country. He also tells you that the dome of the stately State House is covered with a thin layer of real gold!

The Professor and CHIP decide to walk over to the Vermont Historical Society Museum to collect some more facts. Rita, Hugh, and Baskerville choose to wander around the State House grounds. Meanwhile, it is time for you to gather your thoughts and some more information. Fill in the grid with the answers to the clues. When you've found them all, go to the box on page 11.

1. Vermont's oldest covered bridge

2. Name of horse breed that is Vermont's state animal

3. Number of shipwrecks divers explore at the bottom of Lake Champlain

4. Forty gallons of maple sap make one gallon of this.

5. A tree that turns yellow and gold in the fall

6. Small spout hammered into the trunks of maple trees

7. Longest covered bridge in Vermont

8. One of Vermont's best-known ski resorts

**Don't Forget Your Map!**
All the answers to this puzzle can be found on the *back* of your Vermont map.

Did you fill in the grid? Some of the boxes are shaded. Write the letters in the shaded boxes, from the *bottom* to the *top*, on the line below.

_____

On page 28, cross off anyone associated with this item.

# Stinky Shoes

Each year, people from around the country bring their smelliest, stinkiest sneakers to the Rotten Sneaker Competition in Montpelier. It sounds too crazy to be true. You've got to check this one out!

Baskerville's sensitive nose leads the way to the Montpelier Department of Recreation where the contest is going strong. In fact, it's going so strong that the smell almost knocks you over! The judges are looking over the aromatic entries. See if you can figure out the exact number of sneakers that have been entered in the contest. After counting them all, jog over to the bottom of page 13.

Did you count the stinky sneakers in the contest? Use that number to find the correct clue below.

**64 Sneakers?** Change Y to E and change X to D.

**66 Sneakers?** Change L to O and change G to N.

**68 Sneakers?** Change C to I and change U to H.

Now turn to page 29 and change the letters in the secret code.

# Patch Work

Before heading south, the crew decides to return to the Burlington area. They want to visit the Vermont Quilt Festival in Essex Junction. In colonial times, quilts and comforters were made from scraps of fabric arranged in patterns. Today, handmade quilts are one of the crafts for which Vermont is most famous. At the fair, artists from around the state display and sell their most beautiful quilts.

As the crew wanders through the exhibits, CHIP stops to study the quilt patterns. He can see something is missing. Actually each quilt is missing one of its squares. You'll sew up your next clue if you can match the squares with the quilts they belong to. Then check the bottom of page 17.

Did you match the squares to each quilt? There were letters on each one. Write the letters for each quilt in the correct spaces below. Then go to page 29 and

change all _____'s to _____'s and all _____'s to _____'s.
      (quilt 1)     (quilt 2)        (quilt 3)     (quilt 4)

# Take It for Granite

The crew leaves Essex Junction and heads southeast to Barre. The most famous site here is the Rock of Ages quarry. The world's largest quarry covers 50 acres and is nearly 600 feet deep! No wonder Barre is called the "Granite Center of the World."

South of the town the crew visits one of the Rock of Ages quarry sites. While they watch a huge chunk of granite being lifted, you sense some rocky clues ahead. Fill in the grid with names of rocks and minerals. The words are grouped by the number of letters in them to help you. We've filled in one word to get you started. When you're done, check the bottom of the page.

**ORE**

**GOLD**
**TALC**

**BERYL**
**BORAX**
**CHALK**
**CHERT**
**SLATE**

**BASALT**
**GABBRO**
**GYPSUM**
~~**MARBLE**~~

**CALCITE**
**CRYSTAL**
**GRANITE**

The vertical word spells: **M A R B L E**

Did you fill in the grid? Four letters are in shaded boxes. Put the correct letters, from top to bottom, in the spaces below. Then go to page 29 and

change all _____'s to _____'s and _____'s to _____'s.

# SWEET TREAT

After a day at the quarry, the crew decides to find a cozy spot to spend the night. They check into a Vermont country inn that is filled with antiques and knickknacks. After a quiet, relaxing evening, they agree to meet early the next morning.

Just after daybreak, the crew gathers in the dining room for breakfast. Every item on the menu features a Vermont favorite—maple syrup. Some items are made with it. Others taste great with the sweet stuff poured over them.

Some sleepy person must have written out the breakfast menu. All the items are scrambled. See if you can unscramble each choice on the chalkboard on page 19. Then write the letters in th box to order up your next clue.

1. SNAPACKE ___ ___ ___ ___ ___ ___ ___ ___
                 1        2

2. TOELAMA ___ ___ ___ ___ ___ ___ ___
              3              4

3. CREFHN SATTO ___ ___ ___ ___ ___ ___      ___ ___ ___ ___ ___
                    5              6    7

4. TISBISUC ___ ___ ___ ___ ___ ___ ___
                  8

5. FUNFISM ___ ___ ___ ___ ___ ___ ___
                       9

6. FLAWSEF ___ ___ ___ ___ ___ ___ ___
            10

7. CITSKY SUNB ___ ___ ___ ___ ___ ___      ___ ___ ___ ___
                                       11

WE USE ONLY
100% PURE VERMONT
MAPLE SYRUP

MAPLE CANDY

MAPLE CANDY

Did you figure out all the menu items?
There are numbers under some of the letters.
Write the correct letters in the spaces below
and then follow that clue.

Turn to page 29 and

___ ___ ___ ___   ___ ___ ___ ___
 7  11   5   1     4   2   8   6

___   ___ ___ ___ ___   ___   ___ .
 4     9   1   7   3     2    10

# GORGEOUS GORGE

After breakfast the crew hits the road again. They pick up Interstate 89 and drive south to White River Junction. From here it is a short drive west to the next stop, Quechee Gorge. The mile-long gorge was carved by the Ottauquechee River. It is called Vermont's Little Grand Canyon.

A bridge crosses 162 feet above the gorge, but Rita wants a closer look. She leads the crew on a hike down to the river. While they explore the gorge bottom, you can fish for your next clue.

Use your map and the word pieces in the Clue Box to fill in the answers. Be sure to cross off the pieces as you use them. When you're done, cast a look at the bottom of page 21.

## Clue Box

GAR  DE  MONT  HON  LE  TON  PEL  TE  SU  Y  THE

LING  MOUN  BORO  SLA  TAINS  PLE  IER  ON  EY  PA  VER  MA

GE  TLE  BEE  THIR  BUR  LEY  TY  BRAT  BENT

**Don't Forget Your Map!**
Your Vermont map has all the
information you need.

1. This is Vermont's capital.

   ___ ___ ___ ___ ___ ___ ___ ___ ___ ___

2. This is Vermont's state insect.

   ___ ___ ___ ___ ___ ___ ___ ___

3. In 1777, Vermont's constitution was the first to outlaw this.

   ___ ___ ___ ___ ___ ___ ___

4. He discovered that no two snowflakes are alike.

   ___ ___ ___ ___ ___ ___

5. This is the state tree of Vermont.

   ___ ___ ___ ___ ___ ___ ___ ___ ___ ___

6. It is Vermont's largest city.

   ___ ___ ___ ___ ___ ___ ___ ___ ___

7. The first postage stamp was made here.

   ___ ___ ___ ___ ___ ___ ___ ___ ___ ___ ___

Did you fill in all the answers? Now look
at the Clue Box. Some letters are left. Write them in
order in the spaces below. Then

___ ___ ___ ___ ___ ___   ___ ___ ___

___ ___ ___ ___ ___ ___ ___ ___ ___ ___

___ ___ ___   ___ ___ ___ ___ ___ .

# Feathered Friends

After your hike, you return to the road. While in Quechee, Professor Pfeffer wants to visit the Vermont Institute of Natural Science Nature Center. Scientists at the center care for injured birds of prey, such as eagles, falcons, hawks, and owls. Birds that are too sick to be set free get a permanent home at the center.

As the crew gets a close look at the birds, you get close to the next clue. Find the bird words in the word search. Only the words in capital letters are hidden. The words are hidden up, down, backward, forward, and diagonally. After you've "pecked" the right answers, fly to the bottom of page 23.

**AMERICAN** kestrel
**BALD** eagle
**CALIFORNIA** condor
**COOPER**'s hawk
**CRESTED** caracara
**GYRFALCON**
**HARRIS**'s hawk
**MISSISSIPPI** kite
**NORTHERN** harrier
**OSPREY**
**PEREGRINE** falcon
**PRAIRIE** falcon
**RAPTOR**
**RED-TAILED** hawk
**SHARP**-shinned hawk
**SNAIL** kite
**TURKEY** vulture

E R S N A C I R E M A
N O H N R E H T R O N
I T A O L N P Y A R G
R P R A I R I E C E Y
G A P B A L D K R D R
E R G I N O E R E T F
R T E H S I R U S A A
E T Y P D S E T T I L
P L R E O T I E E L C
T E H E H O Y S D E O
Y D E L O G C C S D N
S I R R A H A B I I N
C A L I F O R N I A M

Have you circled all the bird words? Some letters weren't circled.
Write them, in order from top to bottom and from
left to right, in the spaces below.

___ ___   ___ ___ ___   ___ ___ ___ ___ ___

___ ___ ___ ___ ___   ___ ___ ___   ___ ___ ___

___ ___ ___   ___ ___ ___ ___.

# Picture Perfect

Hugh turns the Which Way wheels southwest toward Arlington, Vermont. The famous illustrator Norman Rockwell lived in this town from 1939 to 1953. It is believed that he used local folks for models when drawing scenes of American life.

The Norman Rockwell Museum in Rutland, just north of Arlington, is filled with his prints and illustrations. The Professor picks up a museum guide. It has the names of some of Rockwell's paintings. Write the titles in the spaces on page 25, linking each title by its first letter and last letter. That means you must use the last letter of one title as the first letter of the next. The first title is already filled in. When you've "drawn" the right answers, take a peek at the box at the bottom of the page.

**MUSEUM GUIDE**

STAGECOACH
DOCTOR AND DOLL
SPRING FLOWERS
~~END OF THE ROAD~~
TWO OLD FRIENDS
LAND OF ENCHANTMENT

E N D O F T H E R O A D _ _ _ _ _ _

POST

THE SATURDAY
~~EVENI~~NG POST

Did you put the titles in order? Some of the letters
are circled. Write the circled letters in
order from *last* to *first*:

_ _ _ _ _ _ _

Now cross this famous place off your list on page 30.

**START** →

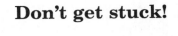
**Don't get stuck!**

# End Game

Your Which Way wandering is nearly over. Your final stop in southern Vermont is Bennington. The historic district downtown is typical of some of the state's most beautiful villages. Many of the buildings date back more than 200 years.

After strolling along the quaint streets, the crew finds a quiet spot to relax. But you have one final piece of work to do. Play the game on this page to complete your adventure. Put a penny or other marker on START. Answer each of the questions and move the marker the number of spaces the answer says. The last space you land on will give you the final clue. Then check the bottom of page 27.

**Cross off the mountains and a quarry.**

**Sniffing the right trail?**

**Don't Forget Your Map!**
All the answers to the questions are on your Vermont map.

**Cross off a cabin and a lake.**

## Keep moving!

1. Where was the first chair lift used?
   a. Mount Snow (move one square)
   b. Mount Ascutney (move four squares)
   c. Mount Mansfield (move two squares)

2. When did Samuel de Champlain claim Vermont for France?
   a. 1924 (move five squares)
   b. 1842 (move two squares)
   c. 1609 (move one square)

3. What direction do you go to get from Springfield to Burlington?
   a. southwest (move three squares)
   b. northwest (move four squares)
   c. southeast (move two squares)

4. Which one of these is NOT a major lake in Vermont?
   a. Memphremagog (move one square)
   b. Passamaquaddy (move three squares)
   c. Bomoseen (move two squares)

5. What is Vermont's nickname?
   a. The Maple Syrup State (move five squares)
   b. Land of Snow (move three squares)
   c. Green Mountain State (move one square)

Now turn to page 30 and do what the final clue says.

**You've got it covered.**

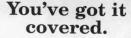

**Cross off a schoolhouse and a mansion.**

**Cross off a rock and the mountains.**

27

**Cross off a quarry and a lake.**

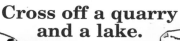

# Who?

Which famous person is going to the Which Way Hall of Fame? Solve the puzzles on pages 2 through 11. Each puzzle will help you eliminate one candidate. When there is only one person left, you will have your answer!

**Andrea Lawrence**
First woman to win two Olympic gold medals for skiing

**Calvin Coolidge**
Thirtieth president of the United States, born in 1872 in Plymouth Notch

**Sinclair Lewis**
First American writer to win the Nobel Prize in literature

**Ethan Allen**
Revolutionary War hero who led the Green Mountain Boys

**Clarina Howard Nichols**
Newspaper editor and early activist for women's rights

**Ben Cohen and Jerry Greenfield**
Friends who started Ben & Jerry's Ice Cream company

**The person going into the Hall of Fame is:**

# What?

One item from Vermont will go to the Which Way Museum. To find out what it is, solve the puzzles on pages 12 through 19. Each puzzle will give you a clue.

Pages 12-13    Change ____ to ____ and ____ to ____.

Pages 14-15    Change ____ to ____ and ____ to ____.

Pages 16-17    Change ____ to ____ and ____ to ____.

Pages 18-19    Change ____ to ____.

Now use the clues to decode the message below; it will tell you how to fill in the picture.

Shade in each space __ __ __ __  __  __ __ __  __ __  __ __.
E C R U  K  R E M  C L  C R

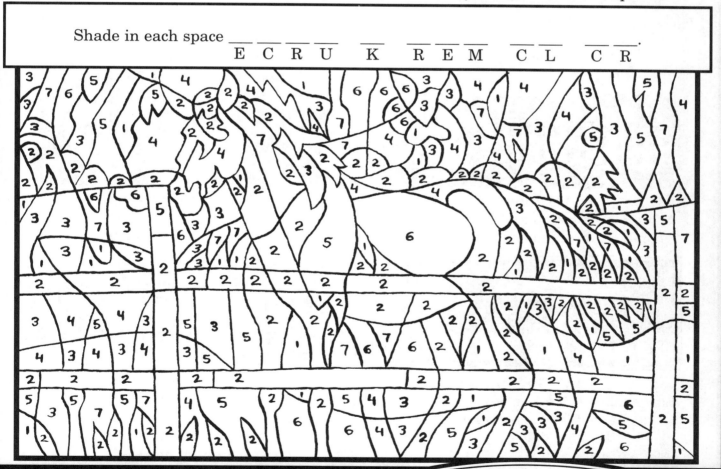

**The item going to the Which Way Museum is:**

# Where?

One landmark from Vermont is to be featured in the Which Way Supermax Movie. To find out where the Which Way cameras are going, solve the puzzles on pages 20 through 27. Each puzzle will help you cross off one or more of the famous places. When you finish, the remaining landmark will be the answer.

### Eureka Schoolhouse State Historic Site
One of the few surviving 18th-century public buildings in the state

### Hildene
A 24-room mansion and former summer home of Abraham Lincoln's son Todd

### Lake Champlain
Large lake on Vermont's western border named for French explorer Samuel de Champlain

### Hyde Log Cabin State Historic Site
Built in 1783 and considered to be the oldest log cabin in the United States

### Green Mountains
Part of the Appalachian Mountain chain that runs through Vermont

### Rock of Ages
Nearly 600 feet deep, 550 feet wide, and a quarter-mile long, the largest granite quarry in the world

**The famous place is:**

All the answers for your
Which Way adventure
are on the next two
pages. Do not go

unless you need help
with a puzzle. If you
don't need help,

before you look at
the answers.

You can use the rest of
this page to work out
your puzzles. If you need
a little extra space,

your pencil here. After
you're done, make a

back to the page you
were working on.

# ANSWERS

## Pages 2-3: **Ski Spree**

Trail 3 goes to the lodge. Eliminate former President Calvin Coolidge on page 28.

## Pages 4-5: **Is There an ECHO?**
In order, the letters on the tags spell ETHAN ALLEN. Cross him off the list on page 28.

## Pages 6-7: **Rebel with a Cause**

1. M U S K E T S
   ‗1‗

2. M A R C H I N G
   ‗2‗

3. R I D I N G
   ‗3‗

4. C A N N O N S
   ‗4‗

5. W A T E R
   ‗5‗

6. T E N T S
   ‗6‗

7. L E T T E R S
   ‗7‗

8. C A R D
   ‗8‗

A N D R E A   L A W R E N C E
4 6 8 3 1 4   7 4 5 3 1 6 2 1

The letters in the numbered spaces spell ANDREA LAWRENCE. Cross the Vermont skier off the list on page 28.

## Pages 8-9: **Moooving Pictures**

There are three hidden milk cartons. Delete Clarina Howard Nichols on page 28.

## Pages 10-11: **State the Facts**

|  |  |  |  |  |  |  |  |  |
|---|---|---|---|---|---|---|---|---|
| ¹P | U | L | P | M | I | L | L |  |
| ²M | O | R | G | A | N |  |  |  |
|  | ³F | I | V | E |  |  |  |  |
|  | ⁴S | Y | R | U | P |  |  |  |
|  | ⁵B | I | R | C | H |  |  |  |
| ⁶S | P | I | L | E |  |  |  |  |
|  | ⁷S | C | O | T | T |  |  |  |
| ⁸K | I | L | L | I | N | G | T | O | N |

When read from bottom to top, the shaded letters spell ICE CREAM. Cross Ben Cohen and Jerry Greenfield off the list on page 28.

## Pages 12-13: **Stinky Shoes**
There are 68 sneakers in the competition. Change C to I and change U to H. Write these letters on page 29.

## Pages 14-15: **Patch Work**
The clue says to replace all R's with T's and all L's with N's on page 29.

## Pages 16-17: **Take It for Granite**

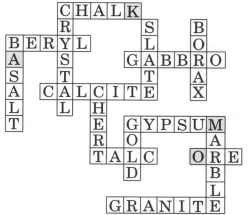

The answer says to change all K's to A's and M's to O's on page 29.